September 1981

To a friend who smiles her troubles away

Martha L. Hensley

TO SEE OUR WORLD

CATHERINE M. YOUNG

TO SEE OUR WORLD

With an essay by Margaret Atwood
and quotations from the
Journals of Henry David Thoreau

WILLIAM MORROW

PRODUCED BY JÜRGEN F. BODEN AND HANS SCHERZ

Layout: Hans Scherz

Library of Congress Catalog Card Number 79-65448

ISBN 0-688-03540-X

Published simultaneously in Canada by GLC Publishers Limited, Agincourt, Ontario and by Les Éditions Fides, Montréal, Québec.

Printed and bound in Canada by Ashton-Potter and Hunter Rose
Color separations by Repro-Wagner, Stuttgart-Kemnat, Germany

ABOUT THIS BOOK

The work of Catherine Young attracted our attention several years ago during the production of a large picture book about Canada. Her nature photography then exhibited motifs of almost classical beauty with fine attention to detail. It presaged an extraordinary artistic talent.

This book is the result of Catherine Young's endeavour to create a collection of photographs to document the beauties of the natural world. The pictures were taken during travels throughout western Canada and the northern United States.

The photographs fire the imagination with the elemental forces of nature captured in wind-tossed trees, delight the eye with the delicate detail of a forest floor and play upon the emotions with sad, snow-shrouded landscapes. They display an artist's intuitive sense of the integrity of the natural world.

Quotations from Henry David Thoreau are used throughout to complement the visual impact of Catherine Young's photographs.

In her introductory essay, Margaret Atwood, internationally known Canadian writer and poet, aptly describes the essence of photography in general, the appropriateness of Henry David Thoreau's prose as commentary, and the particular sensitivity and talent of Catherine Young.

The Editors

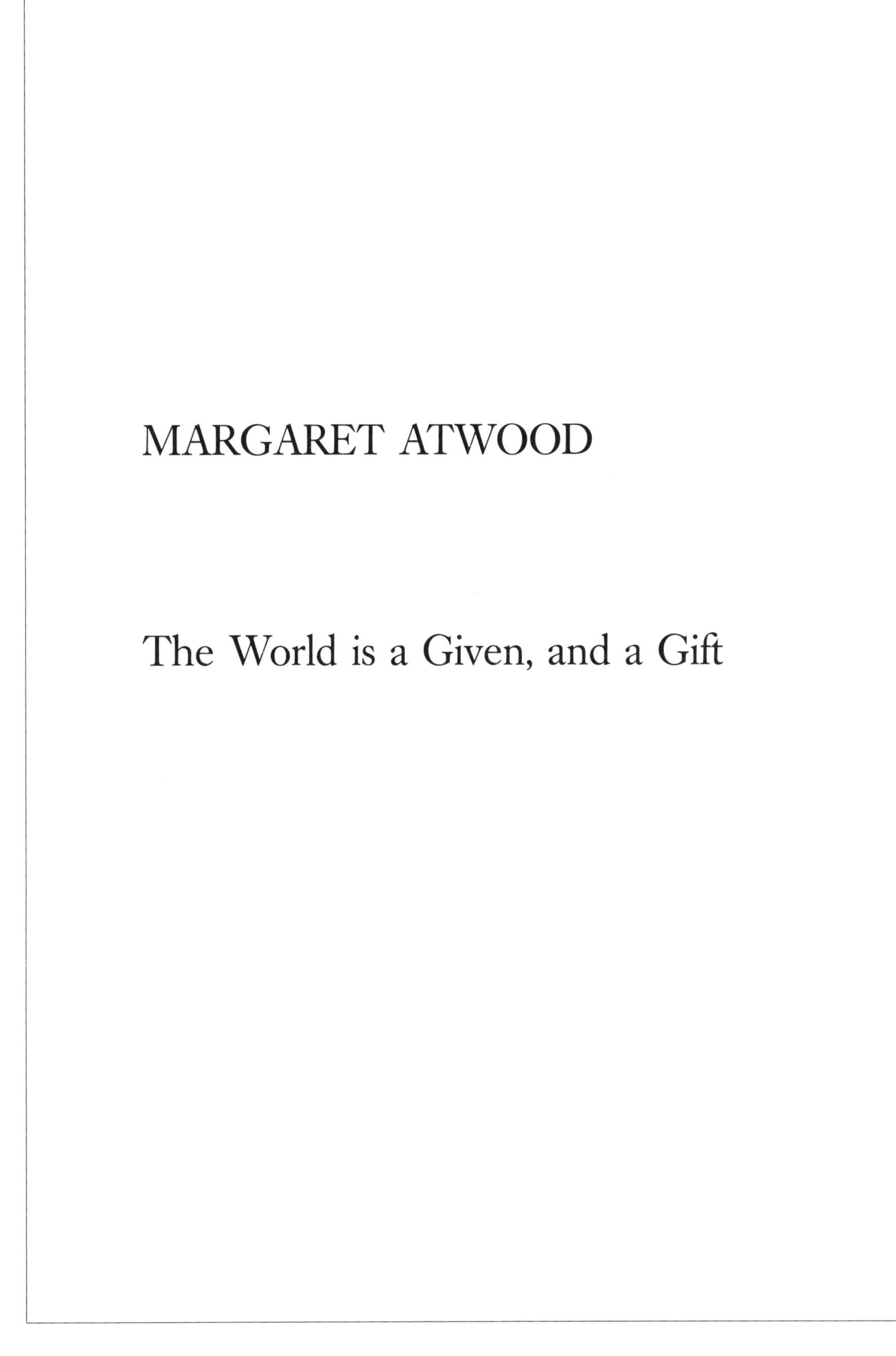

MARGARET ATWOOD

The World is a Given, and a Gift

. . . this natural world is only an image and material copy of a heavenly and spiritual pattern . . . Thus the sage sees heaven reflected in Nature as in a mirror, and he pursues this Art, not for the sake of gold or silver, but for the love of the knowledge which it reveals.

Sendivogius (1750)

Writing an introduction to a book of photographs – especially since this writer knows nothing about photography except that you press a button – is probably an exercise in futility; as futile as an attempt to translate a novel into photographic images. The photograph is frozen light while the printed word is frozen sound: what can one have to say about the other?

In the face of the object itself, which holds its own enigmatic and untranslatable life, the commentator is usually reduced to the rumblings of portentous adjectives or to a precision-drill rundown of techniques.

Refuge for the simple-minded may be sought in a discussion of subject-matter or content; a choice which, in the case of Catherine Young, may at first seem tempting. Her subject is invariably Nature; and the pigeon-hole labelled

Nature Photography gapes open, ready to swallow any photographer unwary or innocent enough to dare a sunset and spit her up again, covered with sentiment. For the photographs made by Catherine Young, such labelling and judgement would be both facile and premature.

It is true that her photographs have a quality which might be called either freshness or innocence: she does not shy away from a sunset if that is what happens to be in front of her. If she lived in a city, she would probably focus its structures through the lens with the same sharpness she now brings to bear on the textures of wood and weathered stone. It is appropriate to mention that she once trained as a biologist and that she now lives surrounded by the things she images (or imagines, outer vision being to a certain type of photographer what inner vision is to a certain type of poet). But for her, the act of making a photograph is less a question of what is being looked at than of how.

Photography, and her photography in particular – a photography that does not rely on darkroom techniques and magician's tricks, which could perhaps be called minimalist in its desire to produce a sophisticated object from the commonest and sparsest of materials – bears something of the same relationship to the visual arts as the found poem does to literature. Both are arts of selection and presentation, rather than what we like fondly to think of as primary creation. By choosing an image, paring away its surround, isolating it, and framing it with the borders of a page, both photographer and poet invite the viewer to see a small fragment of reality in a light that is new to him, to separate it from the flow of less important events, of what is taken for granted.

Of course, such a procedure argues a faith on the part of the artist: that what is there, what is chosen, has enough importance to justify such isolation and framing. The found poet believes that the words he has stumbled across contain a meaning which they will reveal; a photographer such as Catherine Young believes the world itself has meaning. That this meaning is no longer conceived of as intellectual meaning, a "knowledge" accessible through the rational mind, only marks the shift from allegory to symbolism which has occured in Western art and thought over the past few hundred years.

The Puritans who settled North America held that Nature was a book written by God and composed of symbols that only had to be translated to yield moral knowledge. The modern North American artist is more likely to believe that the natural world is composed of symbols, but symbols that can never be fully translated. Hermetic, opaque, the objects so carefully selected and illuminated by Catherine Young nevertheless radiate an energy that communicates without revealing.

It is fitting that Thoreau provides the verbal glosses to this visual text: halfway between the Puritans and modern North America, he, too, regards Nature as a book, though not as closed dogma.

The Nature revealed by Catherine Young's camera is not the nineteenth-century Darwinian world of Tennyson, red in tooth and claw. Nothing devours anything here, nothing is seen to grow or move.

This is a natural world stilled and quiet, displaying a sensitivity that is almost Japanese: Zen photography.

For Catherine Young, the world is what you have to look at and all you have to look at, and photography is the act of learning to look long and well. The world is a given, and a gift.

HENRY DAVID THOREAU

You must live in the present . . .

You must live in the present, launch yourself on every wave, find your eternity in each moment. Fools stand on their island opportunities and look toward another land. There is no other land; there is no other life but this.

Within little more than a fortnight the woods, from bare twigs, have become a sea of verdure, and young shoots have contended with one another in the race. The leaves have unfurled all over the country.

At the same time that we are earnest to explore and learn all things, we require that all things be mysterious and unexplorable, that land and sea be infinitely wild, unsurveyed and unfathomed by us because unfathomable.

We must be refreshed by the sight of inexhaustible vigor, vast and titanic features, the sea-coast with its wrecks, the wilderness with its living and its decaying trees, the thunder cloud, and the rain which lasts three weeks and produces freshets.

I love nature, I love landscape, because it is so sincere. It never cheats me. It never jests. It is cheerfully, musically earnest. I lie and rely on the earth.

A cold and dark afternoon, the sun being behind clouds in the west. The landscape is barren of objects, the trees being leafless, and so little light in the sky for variety. Not a mosquito left. Not an insect to hum. Crickets gone into winter quarters. Friends long since gone there, and you left to walk on frozen ground, with your hands in your pockets.

Nature will bear the closest inspection. She invites us to lay our eyes level with her smallest leaf, and take an insect view of its plain.

The very forest and herbage, the pellicle of the earth as it were, must acquire a bright color, an evidence of its ripeness, as if the globe itself were a fruit on its stem, with ever one cheek toward the sun.

Ah! I need solitude. I have come forth to this hill at sunset to see the forms of the mountains in the horizon, – to behold and commune with something grander than man. Their mere distance and unprofanedness is an infinite encouragement.

Why do the vast snow plains give us pleasure, the twilight of the bent and half-buried woods? Is not all there consonant with virtue, justice, purity, courage, magnanimity?

How long we may have gazed on a particular scenery and think that we have seen and known it, when, at length, some bird or quadruped comes and takes possession of it before our eyes, and imparts to it a wholly new character.

I come to my solitary woodland walk as the homesick go home. I thus dispose of the superfluous and see things as they are, grand and beautiful.

Every fruit on ripening, and just before its fall, acquires a bright tint. So do the leaves; so the sky before the end of the day, and the year near its setting. October is the red sunset sky, November the later twilight. Color stands for all ripeness and success.

The wind sounds like the roar of the sea, and is enlivening and inspiriting like that, suggesting how all the land is seacoast to the aerial ocean. It is the sound of the surf, the rut of an unseen ocean, billows of air breaking on the forest like water on itself or on sand and rocks.

Each phase of nature, while not invisible, is yet not too distinct and obtrusive. It is there to be found when we look for it. Nature is like a silent but sympathizing companion in whose company we can walk and talk, or be silent.

I find it good to remember the eternity behind me as well as the eternity before.

Our appetites have commonly confined our views of ripeness and its phenomena – color and mellowness and perfectness – to the fruits which we eat, and we are wont to forget that an immense harvest which we do not eat, hardly use at all, is annually ripened by nature, fruits which address our taste for beauty alone.

How pleasant to walk over beds of these fresh, crisp, and rustling fallen leaves! How beautiful they go to their graves! How gently lay themselves down and turn to mould! Merrily they go scampering over the earth, selecting their graves, whispering all through the woods about it. They that waved so loftily, how contentedly they return to dust again and afford nourishment to new generations of their kind.

Is not this a language to be heard and understood? There is, in the brown and gray earth and rocks, and the withered leaves and bare twigs at this season, a purity more correspondent to the light itself than summer offers.

Everything is in rapid flux here, suggesting that Nature is alive to her extremities and superficies. But this particular phase of beauty is fleeting. Nature has so many shows for us she cannot afford to give much time to this.

The winter, with its snow and ice, is not an evil to be corrected. It is as it was designed and made to be, for the artist has had leisure to add beauty to use.

When I think of the tragedies which are constantly permitted in the course of all animal life, they make the plaintive strain of the universal harp which elevates us above the trivial.

The season of hope and promise is past; already the season of small fruits has arrived. We are a little saddened, because we begin to see the interval between our hopes and their fulfillment. The prospect of the heavens is taken away, and we are presented only with a few small berries.

Ere long the frost comes out of the ground like a dormant quadruped from its burrow and migrates to other climes in clouds. Thaw with his gentle persuasion is more powerful than Thor with his hammer. The one melts, the other but breaks in pieces.

This restless and now swollen stream has burst its icy fetters and its surface is lit up here and there with a fine-grained silvery sparkle which makes the river appear something celestial, more than a terrestrial river. If rivers come out of their icy prison thus bright and immortal, shall not I too resume my spring life with joy and hope? Have I no hopes to sparkle on the surface of life's current?

We must not expect to probe with our fingers the sanctuary of any life, whether animal or vegetable. If we do, we shall discover nothing but surface still. The ultimate expression or fruit of any created thing is a fine effluence which only the most ingenuous worshipper perceives at a reverent distance.

A lake is the landscape's most beautiful and expressive feature. It is earth's eye; looking into which the beholder measures the depth of his own nature. The fluviatile trees next the shore are the slender eyelashes which fringe it, and the wooded hills and cliffs around are its overhanging brows.

We get only transient and partial glimpses of the beauty of the world. Standing at the right angle, we are dazzled by the colors of the rainbow in colorless ice. From the right point of view, every storm and every drop in it is a rainbow. Beauty and music are not mere traits and exceptions. They are the rule and the character. It is the exception that we see and hear.

I begin to see an object when I cease to understand it and see that I did not realize or appreciate it before, but I get not further than this. How adapted these forms and colors to my eye! I am made to love the pond and the meadow, as the wind is made to ripple the water.

The flowers are widely dispersed, perhaps because the sweet which they collect from the atmosphere is rare but also widely dispersed, and the bees are enabled to travel far to find it; a precious burden which the heavens bear and deposit on the earth.

In this fresh evening each blade and leaf looks as if it had been dipped in an icy liquid greenness. Let eyes that ache come here and look, the sight will be a sovereign eyewater.

At present I am subsisting on certain wild flavors which nature wafts to me, which unaccountably sustain me, and make my apparently poor life rich.

I long for wildness, a nature which I cannot put my foot through, woods where the wood thrush forever sings, where the hours are early morning ones, and there is dew on the grass, and the day is forever unproved, where I might have a fertile unknown for a soil about me.

The mellowest, the ripest, red imbrowned color! It is the autumnal tints in spring, only more subdued and mellow. How sweet is the perception of a new natural fact! suggesting what worlds remain to be unveiled. It is a natural magic. These little leaves are the stained windows in the cathedral of my world.

To him who contemplates a trait of natural beauty no harm nor disappointment can come. The doctrines of despair, of spiritual or political servitude, were never taught by such as shared the serenity of nature.

We are affected like the earth, and yield to the elemental tenderness; winter breaks up within us; the frost is coming out of me, and I am heaved like the road; accumulated masses of ice and snow dissolve, and thoughts like a freshet pour down unwonted channels.

The subtlest, most ideal, and spiritual motion is undulation. It is produced by the most subtle element falling on the next subtlest. The rippling of the waves is a more graceful flight.

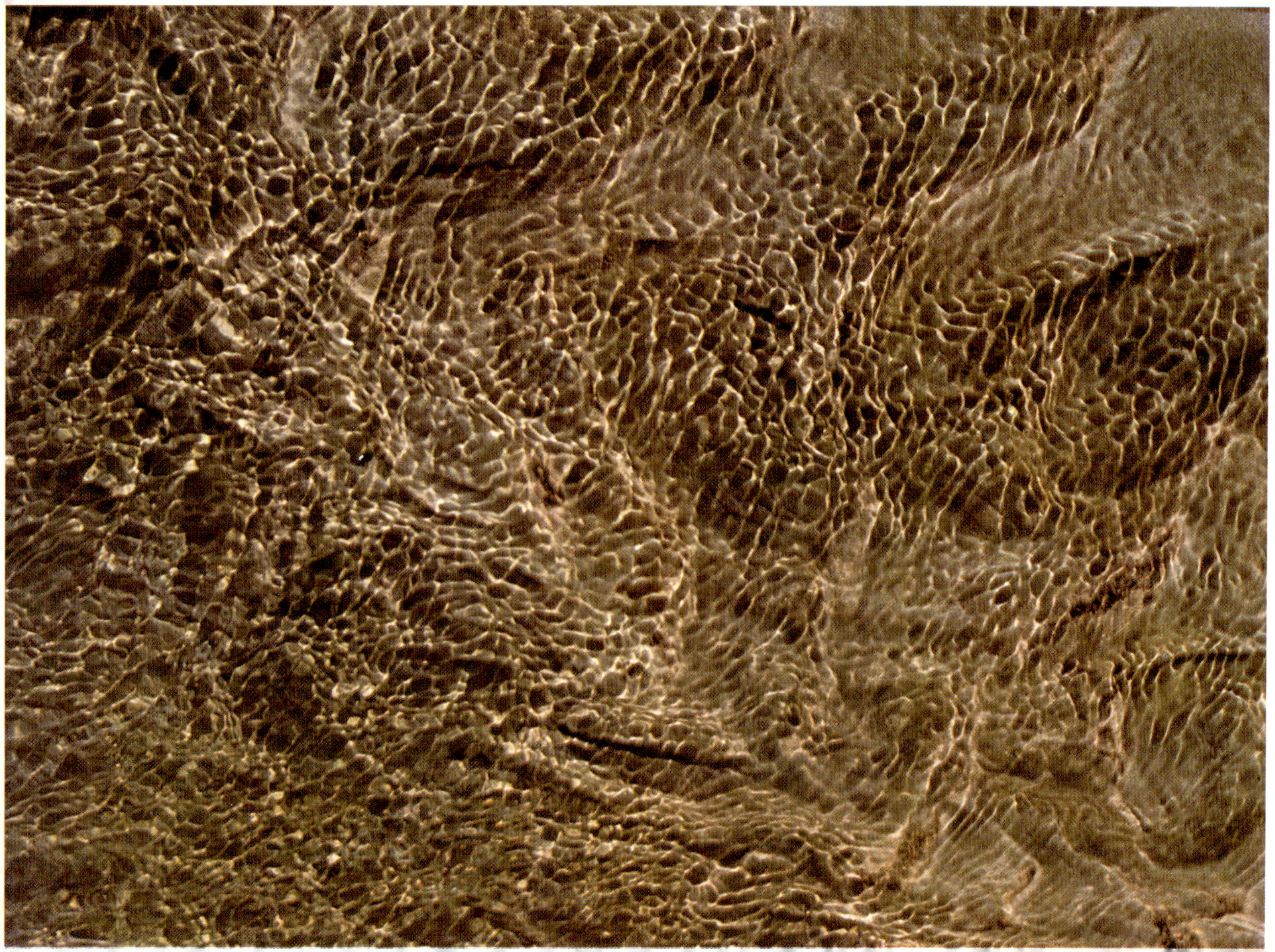

What is Nature unless there is an eventful human life passing within her? Many joys and many sorrows are the lights and shadows in which she shows most beautiful.

All things are subjected to a rotary motion, either gradual and partial or rapid and complete, from the planet and system to the simplest shell and pebbles on the beach; as if all beauty resulted from an object turning on its own axis, or others turning about it.

Nature is constantly original
and inventing new patterns,
like a mechanic in his shop.
When the overhanging pine
drops into the water, by action
of the sun, and the wind
rubbing it on the shore,
its boughs are worn white and
smooth and assume fantastic
forms, as if turned by a lathe.

I know of no object more unsightly to a careless glance than an empty thistle-head, yet, if you examine it closely, it may remind you of the silk-lined cradle in which a prince was rocked.

Rocks which have lain under the heavens so long should be gray, as it were an intermediate color between the heavens and the earth. The air is the thin paint in which they have been dipped and brushed with the wind. Water is still more like it in color. Time will make the most discordant materials harmonize.

I hear the tolling of a distant funeral bell, its serious sound is more in harmony with this scenery than any ordinary bustle could be. It suggests that a man must die to his present life before he can appreciate his opportunities and the beauty of the abode that is appointed him.

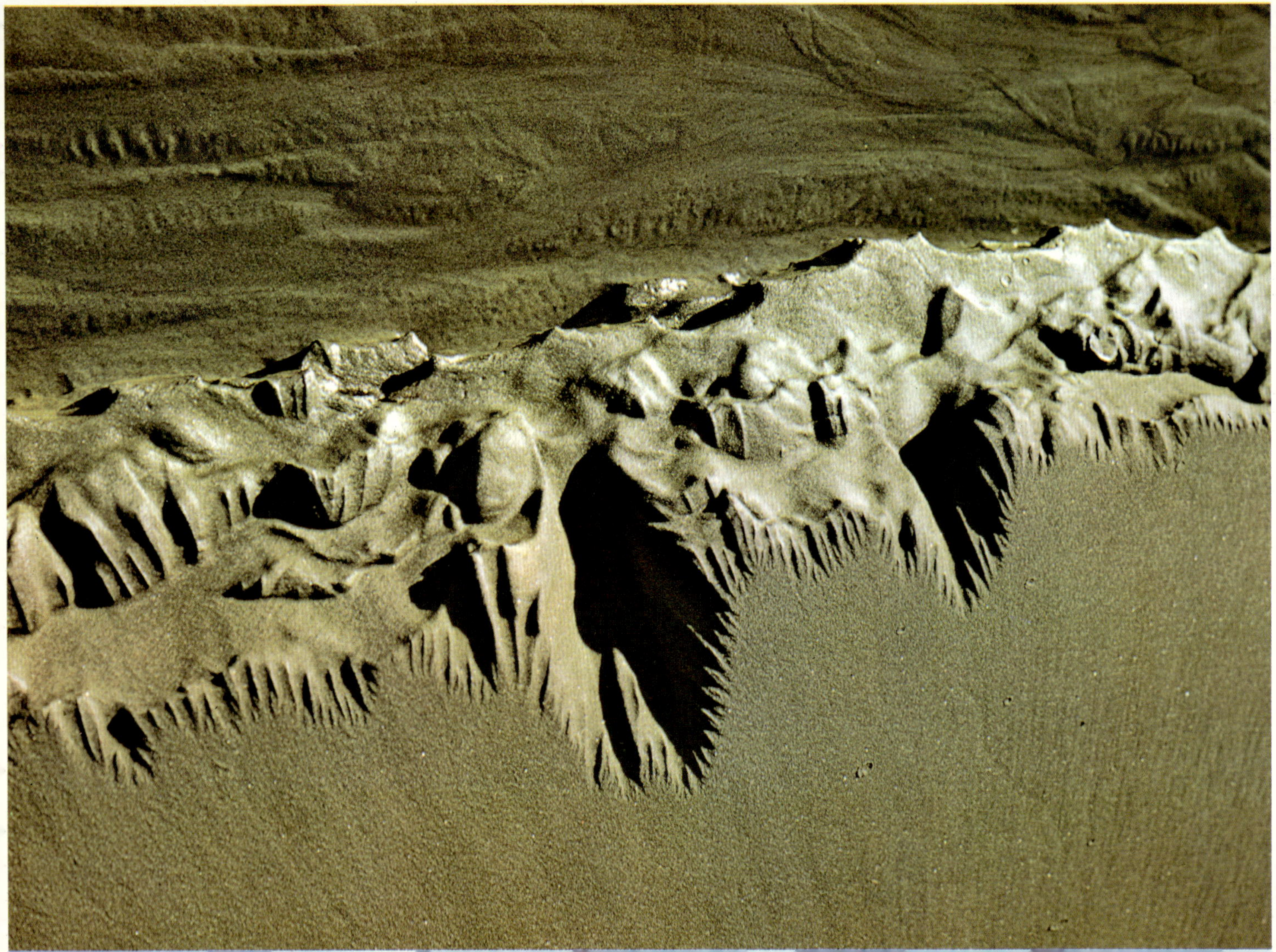

THE PICTURES OF THIS BOOK

All place-names in British Columbia unless otherwise stated.

110	Shore grass, weathered stumpwood
113	Dead thistle leaves, rocks
114	Sea-sculpted rocks, beach, Lucy Island
116/117	Cormorants, Raglan Point, Balaclava Island
119	Pink rock, red cedar, water, sand and seaweed, Burnett Bay
120	Golden stream pattern in sand, Long Beach, Vancouver Island